Emotional Intelligence guidebook

Daily Tips To Master Your - Emotions, Raise Your "EQ", & Become Successful

Written By

Glenn Cummings

Table of Contents

INTRODUCTION

Thank you for purchasing this book!

Congratulations on purchasing this copy of *Empath Healing: The Empath's Survival Guide. Simple And Effective Practices To Become An Energy Healer And Develop Your Mystic Consciousness* and thank you for doing so. Within the following chapters, you'll find a comprehensive guide for empaths of any type, or any level of experience, to channel their empathic gifts into healing. While we will touch briefly on definitions of empathy and the common experiences of those who identify as empaths within the first few chapters, this book will be primarily focused on the process of healing the self and others with your empathic sensibilities. It will be geared towards those readers who have already self-identified as empaths, and are now wondering:

"What comes next?"

"How can I manage my empathic abilities, instead of allowing them to manage me?"

"Will these feelings ever change?"

"Why am I like this?

"Why does everyone else seem to see the world so differently from the way I see (or feel, or know) things?"

"Will things get better for me, with time? Or will they get worse?"

"Does it ever get easier?"

"How can I protect myself?"

"How do I hold onto my strength, energy levels, positivity, and joy in the face of adversity?"

"Now that I've discovered this ability... what am I supposed to *do* with it?"

This being the case, it may be helpful for those who are new to the concept of empathic sensitivity to further research any terms or ideas mentioned in the first three chapters that are mainly foreign, novel, or confusing to them, before reading on.

This book will also be helpful to those who recognize a loved one as empathic and wish to understand their particular challenges and strengths better, or perhaps offer guidance and support to an empath who appears to be struggling. It must be said, however, that an essential step in an empath's journey is learning self-determination; therefore, it is always preferable for developing empaths to read a text like this for themselves, rather than having the information relayed through a third party as advice. Many empaths who have not yet fully empowered themselves will struggle to differentiate between their own feelings and desires, and the emotions and motivations that other people *expect* them to own. Even those who are well-intentioned and full of love for the empath may inadvertently superimpose their own values, beliefs, and judgments into their interpretation of this text, and therefore serve to distort the empath's understanding of these concepts.

By contrast, when an empath is able to read through this book on their own, they'll be far more likely to connect on a personal level and identify the specific emotional experiences that resonate most with them. All empaths have a few things in common, but there is a great deal of diversity within the empath community, as well. Some advice for empaths can be designed from a one-size-fits-all perspective, but not all; physical empaths, for example, may find their healing journey follows quite a different path than that of an emotional or geomantic empath. Likewise, an empowered empath may take a different message away from this book than a repressed, unconscious, or broken empath would. Age, gender identity, race, sexual orientation, personality, profession, and background experience all work in concert to define any empath's perspective on the world around them and their internal landscape. It is crucial for every empath to recognize that they are not alone in their struggles, but that they are each unique and precious as a rare gem. Doing so will allow the empath to overcome the challenges of their sensitivities, rather than viewing them as a shortcoming or curse, and embrace their abilities, looking at them not only as a gift but as a superpower that they would be remiss in keeping hidden away from the rest of the world.

Many empaths carry deep emotional wounds. Often, we are taught from a young age that our sensitivities are unacceptable—that we must hide them, or learn to outgrow them, and disguise our true natures in order to fit in and thrive in an empathy-deficient world. But empaths are natural healers, truth-tellers, emotional and spiritual beacons. The ultimate goal of this book will be to rewrite the story that empaths have been told about themselves by others, in order to help them see their inherent value and reach their full potential. If you have been told throughout your life that you are too sensitive, too intense, too emotional, or just generally *too much*, you may have grown to view your empathic abilities as a fire inside you that needs to be stomped out. My hope is that by the time you finish this book, you'll instead see that fire as one that should be fed because it is a rare point of light in a vast sea of darkness. The world needs you and the fire you carry inside. When you learn to heal yourself, your fire will grow and shine bright; when you learn to heal others, that fire will catch, and your light will spread throughout the world.

There are plenty of books available on this subject, so thank you again for choosing this one. Every effort was made to ensure it is full of as much useful information as possible. Please enjoy!

Enjoy your reading!

A Brief History of

Emotional Intelligence

The state of emotional intelligence as an area of social science today is a result of the trajectory the field has taken since it first appeared in the 1960s. It isn't always easy to trace the path that a social scientific subject has taken, usually because aspects like when a coin was first termed or who the first person was to study the subject are often lost to history. But in the case of EI, we can weave a quilt of where this fascinating subject began and how it changed over time. Indeed, many aspects of the picture of EI that exist today are a result of its unique history.

The study of intelligence became popular in the 19th century as many minds in the Western world began to wonder what precisely it was that made humans unique. Now science tends to use the term exceptional, but at this time, little had been studied in the fields of human behavior and anthropology, or at least little had been documented. As Europeans in the West began to make contact with groups outside of their scope with increasing frequency, they began to question that the picture that they had of human beings and the human experience was still holding true.

Indeed, this period in European history was notable for the Industrial Revolution along with various other political and social movements that were changing the way men and women perceived their world. It was a time of – isms: socialism, nationalism, colonialism, militarism. Essentially, society in the West was changing in ways so drastic that many people would be unconscious of how much things had changed until after the fact. This book certainly is not intended to be a historical review of all the –isms that have influenced the social sciences, but it is important in gaining an understanding of emotional intelligence to get a sense of the antecedents.

Perhaps the single historical event that influenced the preponderance of the –isms was the French Revolution, which fundamentally changed the course of European history. No longer were the ruled expected to tolerate their lot, no matter how many centuries of tradition might be overturned. The men and women of Europe began to expect equal partnership in governance with the aristocrats and monarchs who traditionally had monopolized control structures in the institution of power.

Although these sorts of political ideas may seem peripheral to the discussion of emotional intelligence, they are not. The 19th century was a time of ideas: a period in which people began to question how they saw and experienced the world, in part because the French Revolution had disturbed all of the power structures that had maintained life in a certain shape for centuries. Institutions like the established church, the monarchy, and the legislative arms of government had often restricted education or access to information in order to determine that ideas did not stray from certain norms.

But in the 19th century, several trends began to converge, which led to more people becoming educated, more people traveling and being exposed to foreign languages and ideas, and more questioning of the old order of things. Even the proliferation of scientific and engineering advancements represented a change: the idea that the old way of life perhaps represented oppression while the Industrial Revolution promised to open the door to a new future.

Although the studies of human pathological behavior that eventually gave rise to psychoanalysis may today be considered somewhat traditional and conservative, these early forays in the social sciences created a tradition that has lasted to the present. As close-minded as some of the early ideas in psychology and psychiatry may be, they still represent the grandfathers of modern-day social science. These early social scientists did not assume that social and religious tradition should dictate human understanding. They deeply questioned the world around them and were ready for others like them to hear their hypotheses to facilitate a sort of information exchange.

This was a time when even what we might consider basic human rights were not guaranteed. Governments commonly censored books and newspapers. A wife who ran away from her husband might be locked away in a sanatorium for the rest of her life as she was deemed a madwoman. The times seem repressive to us today, but they were more open than the preceding centuries, and they set the stage for the types of discussions that are had today on common subjects in social science, like intelligence.

It was a man's world, and part of the way intelligence was understood reflected that. The cognitive ability that was associated with the male sex was regarded as representing intelligence while the qualities of women were often regarded as more domestic. Women were considered the fairer sex, while men were believed to be the ones capable of the intellectual work that would spur society forward (toward what, who knew?). Although the early psychologists and psychiatrists did not question these beliefs, the work they did provided an example for perhaps more open-minded social scientists to follow later.

Indeed, the early psychologists and psychiatrists seemed to support traditional beliefs about intelligence and gender rather than to question them. This in part had to do with the fact that psychiatry (and the idea of social science) was still very new in the 19th century. There had certainly been mental wards and asylums in the 18th century, but these were places where men and women were locked away rather than treated or analyzed. The newness of social science in the 19th century is evident in some of the ideas of these early scientists, some of which are part of social scientific canon and others of which are rightly regarded as archaic.

The writings of men like Sigmund Freud, though still interesting to us today, are rife with assumptions about gender and sexuality. Although an examination of where precisely these ideas come from is outside the scope of this book, it is interesting to ponder the idea that many of the basic assumptions of that time have changed. Ideas about certain people perhaps being prone to hysteria while others exhibit pathological sexual desires. These ideas can still be found in the writings of people like Freud: the color the field today, even if most of them now dwell in the hall of disrepute.

These traditionalist ideas in social science carried on into the 19th century. Indeed, the early social scientists really were just scientists who happened to be studying areas that today, most people do not consider to be "hard science." This idea of social science as really just a branch of science is clear in ideas about intelligence that persisted until emotional intelligence and other forms of intelligence began to be studied more actively in the 1980s and 1990s as a result of a number of important books and articles being published.

The point being, of course, that emotional intelligence represented an extremely novel idea in social science because it was born at a time when social science was perhaps beginning to distance itself from science. As social science began to recreate itself as a spectrum of fields of study that was more human or humane than other scientific fields, it stood to reason that investigators in the field would be willing to reexamine not only how science approached ideas like intelligence, but even how social science approached these ideas.

The Beginnings of Emotional

Intelligence

It is believed that the term "emotional intelligence" first appeared in a paper by Michael Beldoch in 1964. It should be obvious to the reader that this was a volatile time in countries like the United States from both a social and an academic standpoint. Civil rights activists were agitating for social change and engaging in protests against the violence that was becoming increasingly commonplace in certain parts of the country. Academics in the scientific and social scientific fields wrote papers that were outright prejudiced or eschewed prejudice. It was the perfect setting for someone to pose the idea that perhaps, ideas that we did not question, like intelligence, really deserved to be questioned.

In 1964, Michael Beldoch wrote a paper entitled, "Sensitivity to the expression of emotional meaning in three modes of communication." This paper is believed to contain the first mention of the term emotional intelligence. In 1966, another paper entitled, "Emotional intelligence and emancipation," by Leuner mentioned the term again. Although it would take another 20 years for emotional intelligence to enter the social science lexicon, these humble beginnings at this critical time helped perhaps establish EI as an idea that was radical and in a good way.

A book by Howard Gardner in 1983 challenged the way that science approached intelligence. This book promoted a theory of multiple intelligences, where interpersonal intelligence and intrapersonal intelligence existed alongside other abilities like traditional cognition and problem-solving. Today, we might think of interpersonal intelligence and intrapersonal intelligence as being similar to self-awareness and social skills in the mixed model of emotional intelligence.

But even in 1983, emotional intelligence remained a term that was still controversial. A dissertation in 1985 mentioned the term again in the context of the study of emotion, while an article for the British Mensa Association in 1987 introduced the idea of the emotional quotient or EQ. Beginning in 1989, models for describing emotional intelligence started to appear. The first was by Greenspan in that year, while another model by Mayer and Salovey appeared in 1990. You will recall that these last two are associated with one of the major EQ tests that is still around today.

Like it or not, much of social science today is impacted by public perception of ideas. This has generally been a good thing as it has contributed to open-mindedness and cultural relativism that is often absent in other sciences. One of the more significant events in the history of emotional intelligence was the release of a book entitled, *Emotional Intelligence – Why It Can Matter More Than IQ*, which helped bring EI to the mainstream.

This book was released in 1995. Perhaps it became so popular (it was a best seller) because there was common societal disaffection with IQ tests, standardized testing in general, pathological approaches to life and living, and a convergence of other social and political trends that had been bubbling over for 40 years (if not longer). The timing of his book just seemed to be right, and ever since the interest in emotional intelligence and the description of it has been on the uptick.

For those curious among you, we can summarize some of the big events in the history of emotional intelligence here:

- 1964: publication of Michael Beldoch's "Sensitivity to the expression of emotional meaning in three modes of communication."

- 1966: publication of Leuner's "Emotional intelligence and emancipation."

- 1983: publication of Gardner's *Frames of Mind: The Theory of Multiple Intelligences*

- 1985: Payne's dissertation, "A Study of Emotion: Developing Emotional Intelligence."

- 1989: publication of Greenspan's model of EI

- 1990: publication of Mayer and Salovey's model of EI

- 1995: publication of Daniel Goleman's *Emotional Intelligence – Why It Can Matter More Than IQ*

Physical Healing Methods

<u>Massage</u>

Massages aren't just about luxury and self-indulgence. A skilled massage therapist—especially one with empathic gifts—can do incredible work to heal discomfort, inflammation, stress injuries, and even some types of organ dysfunction. They can also address emotional issues, like stress, grief, anxiety, or chronic anger.

Training to become a massage therapist usually involves extensive study of human anatomy, allowing the masseuse to gain a thorough understanding of connective tissues, organ systems, and muscular function. Empaths have a competitive edge here, as they can often sense the root of other people's physical discomfort and see a clear pathway to relieving their tension or pain, even without extensive knowledge of anatomic systems.

As is the case with most of the healing arts listed in this text, empaths who choose to either receive or perform massage therapy are advised to strengthen their boundaries and use whatever means necessary—whether it is the creation of an energy shield, or wearing a protective crystal pendant during sessions—to protect themselves from emotional contagion during sessions. There are three primary reasons for this recommendation. First, many people fall into a relaxed and meditative state during a massage session, whether they intend to or not; this meditative energy is powerful, and can forge a deep connection between the therapist and the client on the table, one which is sometimes more intimate than either party desires. Secondly, effective massage can help to release deep-seated tensions, which are often linked to repressed memories or long-stifled emotions. When these issues are brought to the surface, difficult feelings, raw pain, and other typical reactions to trauma permeate the energy field between the client and masseuse; emotional contagion is a serious risk here.

Finally, since many empaths emit warm and caring energy to all people, regardless of the level of intimacy or attraction that exists between them, some clients may misinterpret the meaning of their kind attitude and sensuous touch as genuine romantic or sexual interest. Empaths who work as massage therapists may receive fairly frequent advances, sometimes from clients who genuinely believe the empath is coming on to them, or sometimes from clients who want to take advantage of them or feel entitled to sexual gratification. Many massage therapists work in private spaces, so this may be a real risk for any empath who is still processing a sexually-based trauma or history of personal violation.

Acupressure

Acupressure is similar to massage but incorporates many of the healing theories of acupuncture, a traditional Chinese method of alternative treatment (which is detailed later in this chapter). Rather than running the hands over the body in a soothing way, targeting muscle groups, tendons, and joints, acupressure targets specific points in the body, and exerts intense, focused pressure upon them, often for several minutes at a time, in order to trigger tension release and restore energy flow throughout the body. Typically, the pressure is applied through just one or two fingertips, pressing deeply into the flesh and moving in a restricted circular motion. This pressure is intended to signal the body's natural healing mechanisms and restore its internal regulatory systems.

Acupressure can be performed upon others, or upon oneself. Generally, multiple sessions are recommended to ensure lasting benefits. As compared to acupuncture, acupressure is much easier to learn and begin practicing, as it focuses of only eight primary pressure points in the body (whereas there are upwards of 350 points used in classical acupuncture theory) and is essentially risk free, so long as you only use as much force as can be applied through two fingers.

Empath healers may find some of the theories of acupressure seem natural and instinctive. Physical empaths, in particular, can pick up this skill quite quickly and develop incredible nuance in their appli cation, as they'll be able to sense which pressure points need the most attention in their patients, as well as which might trigger painful or uncomfortable sensations.

Physical Therapy

Unlike most healing forms listed in this text, physical therapy is widely embraced by western medicine and is typically recommended by doctors as part of a post-treatment or long-term recovery process. Those who are ill or injured can benefit from regular physical therapy sessions, retraining their bodies to function optimally, and learning how to manage their pain without prescription drugs.

The goal of most physical therapy is rehabilitation through stretching and various forms of exercise. Physical therapy does not usually address holistic health concerns or explore the ways in which our emotions and mental states impact the function of our organs, muscles, and endocrine systems. Empaths may find that work in physical therapy provides them with many opportunities to provide care, support, and healing insight to those who are most in need, as patients are usually past the point wherein western medicine can offer them any further relief or treatment. They must take care, though, to shield themselves emotionally and physically from empathic contagion, as most of their patients will be in a significant amount of pain and potentially recovering from emotional trauma, as well.

Yoga

These days, many people think of yoga primarily as a form of exercise, but this ancient Indian practice was originally designed as a holistic healing method, promoting harmony between the heart, soul, body, and the divine elements. It is an amazingly versatile tool, accessible to the young and old, rich and poor, regardless of body size, physical fitness level, race or gender. For those who do not put much stock in metaphysical workings, it is still a wonderful way to enhance flexibility and physical balance, build muscle, purge toxins, relieve stress, reduce pain and inflammation, correct poor posture or misalignment issues, and prevent stress injuries. If you are able to embrace the spiritual side of yoga and incorporate meditation, mantras and chakra alignment, crystal healing, or other forms of spiritual or metaphysical energy work into your time on the mat, there is no end to what you might stand to gain from your practice. Yoga can simultaneously address physical, mental, and emotional health issues. It can be humbling and empowering, meditative and playful, awkward, and comfortable, all at once.

Some forms of yoga are slower, milder, calmer, and involve little to no physical exertion; other forms can be faster-paced, with difficult poses and complex sequences of movement. The latter can be extremely physically challenging, and will likely encourage toxin release through heavy sweat. All forms of yoga, no matter how strenuous or relaxing will involve a focus on mindful breathing, with inhalations and exhalations synchronized with specific movements. Any practice that incorporates pranayama will be particularly focused on harnessing the power of our breath, breathing mindfully, and using breath strategically to certain power postures.

Hatha yoga is a great place to start if you're feeling at all intimidated about dipping your toes into the rich, rewarding world of yoga. Hatha classes are highly instructional, leading students through some of the most basic and accessible poses with step by step guidance. A Hatha class isn't likely to get you sweating or to purge too many toxins, but it will help you to improve flexibility, balance, and focus, to reduce your stress levels, and encourage you to feel more comfortable and confident on a yoga mat. It's a wonderful introductory practice, but experienced yogis can also stand to gain a lot by returning to the basics in a Hatha class.

Iyengar yoga is a slow-paced practice that focuses on finding proper and sustainable alignment in every single pose. Teachers typically help their students to achieve ideal alignment despite their own physical limitations by providing props—blankets, blocks, straps, and so on—that help to keep their bodies in the right position. Though the classes move fairly slowly, you may be quite surprised at how exhausted you are by the end of one session, as the practice takes a great deal of physical tenacity and mental focus. Iyengar is a great choice for yogi's healing from an injury or suffering from chronic pain.

Restorative yoga is also a wonderful option for those with pain conditions or anyone in need of a rejuvenating experience. In these classes, most poses are built while lying down on the floor, using props when necessary, to allow yogis to experience deep stretches and realignment without any exertion or strain on the muscles. As in Iyengar, these poses are usually held for several minutes at a time, encouraging deep relaxation and tension release. Classes are usually more soothing and calming than energizing, and they are often offered later in the evenings by low light or candlelight, sometimes including aromatherapy, to help students transition into a restful mode at the end of a long workday or week. Most teachers of restorative and Iyengar yoga are prepared to offer special accommodations or instructions to students with injuries or health concerns.

Ashtanga and Bikram yoga classes may be ideal for yogi's who prefer a predictable routine that they can practice and perfect over time. Ashtanga is a challenging and faster-paced practice that follows the same exact series of postures in every single class. Bikram yoga also follows the same routine

31

sequence in every class, but classes are held in artificially heated rooms to enhance flexibility and toxin release.

If you prefer more variety in your classes, you may instead choose Vinyasa yoga in place of Ashtanga, or a Hot Yoga class over a Bikram class. Vinyasa yoga classes work through a different series of postures in each session, and teachers frequently remind students that it is perfectly fine if they don't catch a pose or two, fall out of rhythm with the rest of the class, or have to bow out for a few minutes and rest in child's pose. Vinyasa moves fairly quickly, but the focus is on fluid, graceful movements connected to the rhythmic breath, rather than on achieving perfect alignment in each pose. Hot yoga classes are similar to Bikram classes; only they offer a varied sequence of poses in place of a standardized routine. Some yogis choose Hot Yoga over Bikram yoga consistently, as the founder of the Bikram style has attracted some controversy since the style was first popularized, and some find his teachings, leadership style, and business practices to involve questionable ethics.

Anusara is a relatively new introduction to the world of yoga, but quite a welcome one. This style is both physically and emotionally restorative, incorporating tantric philosophy to teach the universal principles of alignment. It proclaims that there is inherent goodness in each and every one of us, and uses postures in combination with mantras, affirmations, and other tools to encourage students to open their hearts and interact with the world through the lens of love, tolerance, and positivity. Anusara is an interdisciplinary style that requires full involvement of the physical, emotional, mental, and spiritual bodies. It is physically similar to the Vinyasa style but looks at the practice in a more holistic and spiritual way.

There are many other yoga traditions and styles, from Jivamukti or Kundalini yoga (which incorporate chakra alignment work and chanting of mantras) to naked rooftop yoga classes. Each style has its own unique set of benefits to offer students, and there is no reason why you should not incorporate multiple schools of thought into your own yoga practice.

Many people are intimidated by the face of yoga that they see in popular culture and social media, where the focus seems to be on complicated, acrobatic poses and a strangely materialistic, competitive, cult-like culture. Some yoga studios do indeed market a version of this ancient practice that is more focused on physical beauty than internal health or emotional well-being and promotes exclusivity over inclusivity, with very little attention drawn to the meditative or spiritual side of yoga. Even so, there are still plenty of studios and independent teachers that honor yoga as a healing art, respecting its oldest traditions and targeting the poses that offer the greatest emotional and physical benefits to their students, rather than those poses that look most impressive in an Instagram post. It is wise to try a few different teachers and studios that offer varied forms of yoga before settling into a routine so that you can find a practice that truly serves you. If you are unable to find a teacher who fulfills your needs, it may be time to consider enrolling in a teacher training course and becoming the kind of teacher you wish you'd been able to learn from! These days, yoga classes can be held in established studios, in homes, in public places, in the great outdoors, and even on the internet, so as a certified teacher, you can impact as few or as many lives as your ambition and drive will allow you to.

Energy Healing

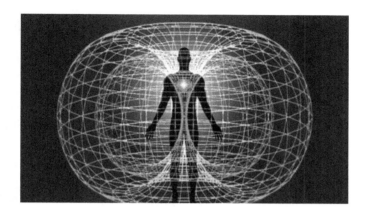

There are many different forms of energy healing, and we'll only touch on some of the most popular forms in this text. Energy healing works to treat the individual's physical, emotional, mental and spiritual bodies all as one, respecting each as interconnected entities that are all impacted by one another, and which should not be compartmentalized or treated separately. It is most effective when all parties involved—both the healer and the recipient of healing energy—are willing to believe and invest emotional energy into the process. Here, we'll detail two of the most well-known forms of energy healing: Reiki and Chakra work. Bear in mind, though, that there are many alternatives to these specific traditions, and endless possibilities if you should choose to combine two or more energy healing strategies.

Reiki

Reiki is an ancient Japanese tradition of energy healing. It works to channel "ki," which is a flowing, energetic life force, through the three "tandens," or centers of energy, in our bodies. The first tanden is found in crown or forehead (in the same place as the third eye chakra, detailed further in the next section of this chapter) and connects us to heavenly energy; the second is the heart tanden, located in the center of the chest, which connects us to human energy, or emotional energy; the third, and most vital of the three, is referred to as "hara," found in the gut, below the belly button, and is the source of both earth energy and "Original energy." Original energy is a term that describes what makes you the person you are: your soul, your purpose, your life path, your essence, and your destiny.

Ki is described as a fluid, everchanging substance that flows in and out of our metaphysical bodies; we do not maintain a fixed amount of ki throughout our lives, but rather, the amount we harness fluctuates in relation to the way we treat ourselves and the manner in which we interact with the world around us. When ki is low, our life force is weakened, and we are more susceptible to illness, discomfort, burnout, emotional dissociation or anguish, and anxiety. When a person has a high level of ki, they are happier, healthier, more energized, motivated, and ready to thrive. Like oxygen, there is an unlimited amount of ki available in our world; the purpose of Reiki is to make sure the body is breathing it in deeply enough to experience all its beneficial effects. Since there is no limit to the amount of ki available for channeling, Reiki is a wonderful healing tool for empaths who are especially susceptible to energy depletion, because it allows the healer to channel energy from the universe, rather than drawing energy from their own metaphysical bodies. There is also a low risk for emotional contagion in an attunement session, as the Reiki master channels ki directly from God; like an empty glass vessel transporting water, the master's personality and current mood do not impact the nature of the spiritual energy flowing into the receiver.

Reiki attunement is not only used for healing physical discomfort; it is also used to combat stress and promote relaxation on both physical and metaphysical levels. Reiki is also a tool used to encourage spiritual growth. It is often spoken of as a gift from God. However, Reiki is not associated with any particular religious dogma. This makes it accessible to people from all cultures and faiths. It can only help, and it can never cause harm.

Compared to some other forms of energy healing, such as Chakra cleansing work, Reiki is an easily accessible healing style to receive as treatment and learn to perform yourself. Anyone can become a Reiki healer—all they really need to get started is initiation, or purposeful transfer of healing energy, from an established Reiki master. This can take place during a healing session, and it isn't a very time-consuming process. After one single attunement and teacher-to-student energy transfer, you will be ready to start healing others with your own ki energy.

Reiki is a natural and safe healing practice, one that poses no potential health risk at all to those who receive attunements. To the casual observer, it may simply look like a gentler, low-contact, and low-pressure version of a massage. The master uses what is called "palm healing" or "hands-on healing" to transfer and balance energy within the receiver's body. The practice is generally quiet and soothing. It can be used in combination with other forms of energy healing (crystal work, meditation, soul retrieval, and more) to optimize and personalize the recipient's healing experience.

If you're not sure whether or not Reiki should be a part of your healing practice, the best way to learn more is to contact a Reiki master and sign up for an attunement. Reiki is something that has to be experienced in order to be fully understood; words fail to describe its power for healing and growth.

Chakra Cleansing and Alignment

Chakra work has several similarities to Reiki; though this healing tradition originated in India rather than Japan, it is entirely possible that both practices evolved from a unified source of truth, translated through different cultures and languages.

In Chakra's work, "kundalini" is the vital energy that vibrates through all living, celestial, and metaphysical bodies. It is the life force that drives us and connects us all; it is the energy that flows through all of the chakras in our bodies, rooting us to the earth while simultaneously linking us to the divine. Some visualize kundalini as a physically ineffable spiritual energy; others picture it as a bright, vibrant light in liquid form that can flow through our chakras most efficiently when they are well aligned and balanced. Kundalini is sometimes characterized as "serpent power," coiled around the root chakra, or as the "sleeping goddess" within who is awakened when the chakras are all aligned and channeling energy in concert.

The word "chakra" means "wheel" in ancient Sanskrit, so each of the seven chakras is depicted as a wheel made of spinning energy, like a whirlpool, inside the body, found at various points along the spinal column. Each chakra is connected to different body parts and organ systems; each has its own emotional and mental health component; each is related to a different element, color, symbol, and resonating sonic frequency. People typically talk about chakras falling out of balance, but this term is often an overgeneralization. Chakras can also be clogged, or too open; they can be reversed, spinning energy in the "wrong" direction, as compared to the others housed in the same body; they can be dormant, or overactive. Each type of dysfunction presents through different symptoms or manifestations. It's also important to remember that the chakras are meant to function as a whole system, so there are no playing favorites with them; focusing on one chakra to the detriment of others will only encourage further imbalance, discomfort, and dysfunction.

Though chakra work is an ancient healing art, with roots deeper in history than our modern understandings of anatomy and medicine, it may appeal even to those who are the most skeptic of the metaphysical, because the seven chakras are a shockingly accurate reflection of our endocrine systems.

An endocrine system is a group of glands that control hormone release within our bodies, and hormones dictate just about every aspect of our lives, from our sleeping and eating habits to our moods and energy levels.

Healing work for any of the seven chakras is often a holistic effort. It may involve recommendations of dietary changes, specific types of movement (sexual activity, for example, or dance), altered sleep habits, particular yoga poses, lifestyle changes, talk therapy, massage, or another form of energy healing. These recommendations may sometimes seem outlandish, such as the suggestion to wear more of a certain color—red for the root chakra, green for the heart chakra, and so on—to restore balance, or to use specific crystals to channel energy to the chakras that need attention. Remember to keep an open mind as a patient, student, or practitioner of chakra alignment work. It would be a shame to miss a healing opportunity for the sake of honoring skepticism, doubt, or disbelief.

All chakras are equally important in healing work, but empaths especially may wish to focus on balancing their solar plexus chakra, which is found in the stomach. The solar plexus chakra is where we house our emotions, or egos, our sense of self-esteem and confidence in our abilities. Most empaths struggle to keep this chakra properly energized throughout their lives, as they have far more emotions to process than the average individual, and they often pour so much energy into others that they never manage to build a stable sense of self.

There are seven major chakras, which are most commonly referenced in energy healing work, but if you wish to dive deep into this practice, you might want to study the minor chakras as well, of which there are an additional five. The twelve-chakra system may be of special interest to geomantic empaths, as it focuses on grounding the balanced body and connecting it to the earth.

Sound healing

Sound healing is also sometimes referred to as "vibrational medicine." It employs various sonic tools, including the human voice, tuning forks, Tibetan singing bowls, digeridoos, gongs, and others, to target specific vibrational frequencies that will encourage relaxation, pain relief, and healing.

Sound is a physical element; if you've ever been to a rock concert and felt the bassline thrumming through the floor, into your feet, legs, gut, and chest, then you know how certain notes and volumes can impact a person's physical and emotional body immediately. We also feel sonic vibrations inside our bodies whenever we speak or sing, though most of us have grown so accustomed to these feelings that we've learned to ignore them. Through sound healing, we can grow to be more mindful of these sensations, and eventually come to use them in strategic manners to impact our energy levels, psychological patterns, and pain management routines.

Music and other forms of sound can impact brain function, altering our moods, helping us to wake up or fall asleep, providing energy or promoting tension release. The theory of sound healing has primarily gained popularity in the last few decades, but threads of this theory can be traced back to a number of ancient healing traditions. In Chakra's work, for example, each energy center in the body corresponds to a particular mantra sound, which patients are often encouraged to chant or sing during their healing sessions in order to channel energetic vibrations to certain areas of the body. The employment of music for healing purposes was also popular in Native American and ancient Egyptian healing traditions.

Empaths may choose to use sound healing in one-on-one meetings with clients, in group sessions, or within the frame of a multidisciplinary healing environment. Sound healers can work with shamans, yoga instructors, Reiki masters, or massage therapists to enhance their efficacy in healing; or, alternatively, they might choose to simply create music with healing vibrations that can be performed, recorded, and enjoyed by believers and non-believers alike.

Acupuncture

Acupuncture is an alternative medicinal practice that originated in China thousands of years ago and is still popularly used today throughout the world. It is a practice in which extremely thin needles are pushed into the skin at various points throughout the body. The needles are usually only inserted to reach a depth of about 1-2 millimeters below the skin's surface, but in some cases, they can go several inches deep. The process is typically not painful, though; the points at which the needles are inserted are acupoints, just like those targeted in acupressure, and when they are gently prodded with these hair-thin needles, they help to release tensions, purge toxins from the body, promote healing and relaxation. Many patients are lulled to sleep in acupuncture sessions; the most intense level of pain they might experience is similar to that of a deep-tissue massage, and the pain is typically fleeting.

Acupuncture theory has some similarities to that of Reiki and Chakra alignment; it focuses on restoring balance and function of vital energy called "qi" which can cause emotional and physical health problems if clogged, imbalanced, or otherwise dysfunctional. Qi should flow freely from the internal organs to the surface layer organs, like the skin, along lines called "meridians." In acupuncture, needles are usually placed along the meridian lines in order to reach the deeper organs connected to them.

Empaths are well-suited to this healing art, primarily because the ability to determine where acupuncture needles are placed often rests on the practitioner's ability to read a patient's energy field. Some acupuncturists determine the placement of needles in a method that is similar to Reiki, hovering their hands over the body or placing them gently upon the skin, and waiting for disturbances in the patient's energy field to physically trip them up or alert them in some other way (visually, sonically, or perhaps even triggering a physical sensation within the practitioner's body). However, this is not a practice that can be winged or performed on the fly; most countries in the world require acupuncturists to acquire licenses from regulatory boards before seeing their own patients, a process which involves thousands of hours of training and education.

Homeopathy

Homeopathy is an alternative to traditional western medicine. Established in the late 1700s, its theories rest upon the notion that our bodies have the ability to heal themselves without much intervention on our part, and that in order to encourage specific forms of healing, we can introduce extremely small amounts of substances that would serve to promote illness in larger quantities. This theory is similar to that of vaccines: by introducing a minuscule, heavily distilled amount of unwelcome substance to the body, we can trigger the body's natural autoimmune responses.

There is a great deal of skepticism as to the effectiveness of homeopathic remedies within the world of western medicine, but in some cases, homeopathy has proven itself to be an effectual element in alternative healing journeys. Empaths may be particularly capable in this field, as the determination of which diluted substances should be prescribed to any patient rests heavily upon acquiring and evaluating detailed information about the patient's life—likes, dislikes, disposition, diet, emotional circumstances, past illnesses and injuries, and aspects of their daily routine.

There are homeopathic remedies available to treat a vast array of illnesses and emotional upsets, from the common cold to a spell of grief. Homeopathy can be combined with any number of other alternative medicine theories to promote holistic healing and restore internal balance.

Naturopathy

You might think of naturopathy as an umbrella term, one which can encompass various forms of alternative healing. The basic premise of naturopathy is that healing from all sorts of maladies and injuries can be accomplished without the use of modern drugs or invasive surgeries. Naturopaths design healing regimens that include exercise, dietary changes, massage, and sometimes even emotionally based recommendations (for instance, someone suffering from an ulcer might be advised to change their career or end a relationship that is causing them stress).

Empaths can make wonderful naturopaths because they are able to see both minor details and the big picture. They will be able to help their patients make changes that are not only necessary and beneficial, but also sustainable because they'll be able to understand the patient's individual capabilities and challenges, strengths, and weaknesses, and so on. The goal of naturopathy isn't short-term healing; it aims to create lasting lifestyle changes that will ensure a balance between the physical and emotional bodies and allow both to function optimally throughout a patient's life. Naturopaths often help to connect their patients with experts in various fields of alternative medicine, such as acupuncturists or homeopaths. Empathic naturopaths can be particularly adept in this area, as they'll be able to predict which practitioners will be a good fit for their patients, and help to foster connections between them, as well as between healers who might work well together.

Ayurveda

Ayurveda is one of the oldest holistic healing traditions in the world. This Hindu practice promotes good health through very specific recommendations of when and what to eat, how much to sleep, how to exercise, and even how to breathe. It looks at the mind, body, and soul as inextricably linked, and believes that good health can only be achieved by finding a balance between all three of these elements. It is generally considered a preventative health measure, rather than a healing strategy. Most practitioners would not recommend it as a cure for cancer, but some believe it can help to prevent or delay the onset of diseases.

Ayurveda is Sanskrit for "the science of life." As such, it is a fairly complex school of thought which requires extensive study to grasp fully. It makes some generalized recommendations, such as the consumption of whole, unprocessed foods and frequent movement of the body—but Ayurveda also recognizes that each individual is unique, and their needs will vary based on circumstances. A practitioner will typically make a detailed evaluation of a patient's physical, mental, and spiritual health before offering any prescribed treatments or lifestyle changes.

Empaths may find the study and practice of Ayurvedic theory to be particularly rewarding, as it offers them the ability to connect with patients on multiple levels and design unique healing plans for each client.

Mental and Spiritual
Healing Methods

Grounding

Grounding, like meditation, is one of the easiest and most accessible healing methods available to those with limited financial resources. It is a wonderful option for those who are short on time and need to maintain emotional balance and energy levels in the face of intense stressors.

All one needs for grounding is a willingness to spend some time outdoors, connecting to nature physically through skin contact. The most basic form of grounding is to walk, or stand, barefoot on natural earth, be it a patch of grass, a sandy shoreline, or a rocky cliffside. Some choose to incorporate yoga into their grounding practice, standing in Mountain Pose (Tadasana), sitting in any variation of Lotus Pose (Padmasana), or lying down in Corpse Pose (Shavasana) to connect with the earth. With skin contact established, take some time to practice mindful breathing; taste the air around you; check in with every physical and emotional sensation currently being held in your body, and accept them for what they are.

Now close your eyes, and check-in with the ground beneath you. How does it feel? Warm or cool? Moist or dry? Smooth or rough? As you breathe naturally, consider all the elements that led this ground to feel exactly as it does beneath your feet. Is it shaped by the winds and waters around it? Does it bask in the sun's light and soak up all its energy, or does it take respite in the shade of a nearby tree? Think of all the myriad ways this particular piece of earth is at one with all the elements surrounding it.

Now, with your eyes still closed and your breathing steady, picture yourself—your aura, your energy, your soul's entire being—as another one of these natural elements, like air, or water, or the warmth of the sun. Picture your energy flowing down into the ground like water into a well, and picture the energy of the earth rising up and flowing through your body, in turn. Imagine yourself growing roots like a tree, feeding off the earth's energy and replenishing that energy with gratitude. Recognize that you are connecting to the earth, and impacting it, shaping it, just as the wind and rain and sun do. This experience should be empowering and humbling, all at once; it should help you to feel that you are a part of something much larger and greater than yourself, but also that you are a vital component of the universe's energy.

Regular grounding is recommended for anyone who suffers from chronic imbalance or disturbance of the root chakra, as it will work to reinforce the notion that the universe will hold you up, if you should fall, and remind you that no matter what happens with your family, friends, co-workers or lovers, you belong; you are worthy; you are impactful; and you are enough, just as you are. Those who are feeling particularly drained or depleted may stand to gain the most from grounding in full, direct sunlight, during the early afternoon hours when the ground has had adequate time to soak up the sun's energy and warmth.

Crystal Healing

Crystals can be incorporated into almost any type of energy healing practice. They can also do powerful work on their own, either when worn or placed strategically in crystal grids. Each type of crystal possesses its own unique set of metaphysical properties; some are recommended for deflecting negative energies, while others absorb or nullify them; some may enhance mental clarity or promote self-confidence; some might be particularly useful in trauma recovery or certain types of pain management. Specific stones are related to each of the seven chakras to target health concerns and correct misalignment.

Here is a list of crystals that are particularly recommended for empaths, and the reasons why they might be useful to you. There are many, many more that you may find resonate with your individual needs.

- Hematite – Soothes and helps you to stay centered; shields against energy depletion

- Apache Gold – also called "healer's gold," this stone helps to strengthen boundaries and encourage clear, honest communication

- Labradorite – Enhances intuition, promotes emotional stability and creativity

- Malachite (polished only) – Clears emotional clogs, promotes the release of tension and negative emotions, neutralizes negative energies from technology sources

- Black tourmaline – Deflects negative energies and channels them into the earth for transformation; protective stone, especially recommended for geomantic empaths

- Carnelian – Promotes physical healing, targeting metabolic function and circulation; empowers and restores self-confidence, as well as a sense of capability

- Citrine – Enhances the function of the solar plexus chakra and the digestive organs; purges emotional blockages and shields against negativity.

- Amethyst – Strengthens intuition, cleanses the aura, and promotes harmony and peace.

Whatever crystals you choose to wear or use in your energy healing practice, be mindful of the fact that crystals need to cleansed regularly. This can be done through smudging, bathing your crystals in the light of a full moon, or even burying them underground overnight before retrieving them. Furthermore, be conscious of the properties of any crystals you choose to use in concert; if their energies work in opposing directions, they may end up nullifying each other's powers.

Shamanic Healing

Shamans are spiritual beings who can translate the messages of the divine for acceptance in the human realm, and vice versa. The tradition of shamanism is ancient and derived primarily from indigenous groups, but there is a growing wave of neo-shamanism, in which modern practitioners are able to design their own spiritual practices, incorporating some ancient traditions while weaving in some of their own inventions.

Shamans are religious leaders who may use their power to heal, communicate with non-human spirits, and even cross back and forth over the line between this world and the afterlife. They are able to guide individuals through intense spiritual journeys that involve ritualistic practices, and sometimes the use of hallucinogenic substances.

A shaman can help to guide your spirit on a number of journeys, including, but not limited to:

- **Soul Retrieval** – A process in which is very similar to the process of reconnecting with your core identity or authentic self as outlined in chapter 4, but achieved through spiritual rituals rather than practical measures. This journey is focused on reclaiming the part of the soul that is lost through traumas in early life and returning to a place of fulfillment.

- **Cutting off ties** – This is similar to the Cord Cutting ceremony referenced in chapter 7, however it can be used to release you from the grip of addictions or toxic behavioral patterns, as well as interpersonal relationships.

- **Past life regression** – This journey is never to be taken lightly and should not be fulfilled simply to satisfy curiosity. A past life may be visited in order to heal from traumas that took place before your lifetime, or to uncover hidden truths from the past that still inform your current identity.

- **Journeying** – A shaman may escort you on a journey into the spirit world, to achieve various forms of enlightenment and personal growth.

Prioritizing Self-Care

Hopefully, by this point, you've been able to select a few healing methods that appeal to your sensibilities. With your empathic gifts thriving, there is no limit to what you might achieve once you make the decision to chase your dreams and spread your healing light.

Still, no matter how far you've come in this journey, it is never a bad time to remember to put yourself first. As a healer, you'll be surrounded by people whose needs will seem more urgent, more important, more vital, than your own. In these situations, your compassionate nature will work against your better judgment, and the temptation to push yourself beyond your own limits may be overpowering.

One great way to protect against this is to establish your self-care routine and engrain it into your schedule and your relationships *before* you dive into healing work. You might even make a list of your self-care needs and review it regularly, like a check-list, to ensure you are continually respecting your own limits and putting yourself first.

Here are some common self-care needs of empaths to inspire you. These items may not all resonate with you, and you might find you have plenty of needs that aren't listed. Draw up a list for yourself, and make it as long or as short as you like. Remember, no one can ever know you as well as you know yourself, and no one else can define how much self-care or self-love you deserve to shower yourself with.

- Space for honest and open emotive expression – We empaths feel things very deeply. If we are immersed in an environment where our emotions aren't welcome—where tears or anguish need to be hidden away—we eventually learn to doubt ourselves and the validity of our emotional responses. Give yourself permission to back away from relationships or environments that consistently put you in the position of having to swallow, mitigate, or lie about your feelings. Work to build a support system of people who also value emotional authenticity and are not frightened by deep, intense feelings. Trust me; they're out there!

- Alone time – Even if your friends and colleagues are the loveliest of people, as an empath, you may feel the urge to hide from the world every once in a while. This is perfectly natural and nothing to be ashamed of. In fact, you might grow to feel a lot more positive about these reclusive spells if you schedule them regularly and plan them out, rather than waiting until you feel so overwhelmed by life that you simply cannot convince yourself to leave your bedroom. Alone time can be restorative, productive, and fun, so long as you save yourself enough energy to be able to enjoy it.

- Adequate rest – Empaths may have extraordinary gifts, but we are still human, and therefore, we need to make sure we get enough sleep in order to function. You may also need to schedule some downtime for yourself that is separate from your sleep schedule or your alone time—time that is unscheduled, devoid of stressors or sources of anxiety, with which you can do whatever you choose. Read a book, reorganize your sock drawer, bake some cookies, or go for a walk with a friend. These activities can be restorative, just like a good night's sleep.

- A health-focused diet – Since so many of us have trouble with our solar plexus chakra and digestive organs, it can be lifechanging to place some firm boundaries around your eating habits. Others will constantly pressure you to abandon these, primarily because your dedication to healthy eating will make them feel guilty for eating haphazardly and irresponsibly. Don't let others sway your decision to give your body the fuel that it needs. It's never worth it to suffer from indigestion, stomach cramps, or emotional turmoil, just to make someone else feel better about their own dietary choices.

- Physical comforts – Others might call you needy, picky, high-maintenance. So what? As an empath, you are more sensitive than most to changes in temperature, itchy or uncomfortable synthetic fabrics, lights, sounds, and scents. Maybe what you really need to feel comfortable is a full outfit made of organic cotton, a thermostat set at precisely 71 degrees, natural sunlight, the scent of lavender essential oils, and some music that is quiet—but not too quiet. Find time and space wherein you can feel entitled to all the things that make you comfortable. Revel in it. You only get one life. Why spend it being uncomfortable, just to avoid judgment from other people?

- Fairness and reciprocity – We all have relationships in our lives that feel a little unbalanced at times. One thing that empaths tend to forget, though, is that if we fill our lives up with these kinds of relationships, we don't leave any room for the kinds of relationships we *do* want. A great way to care for yourself and stop toxic emotions like resentment from flourishing inside you is to address injustices or one-sided relationship behaviors immediately before they can spin out of control. If you never allow someone to take advantage of your kindness, then you never have to deal with feeling resentful down the line. Work to surround yourself with people and institutions that also value fairness and reciprocity. When you stumble into those that don't, there's no reason to waste your energy in fighting them; just walk away, and channel your energies into finding a better place to be.

- Authenticity and sustainability – Empaths thrive best when they build lives for themselves that are centered around honesty, real connection, and forethought. Lies and inefficient systems stick out to us like sore thumbs, and while most people can shrug these things off, we often find them impossible to ignore or tolerate. As such, you may derive a great deal of peace of mind by investing in authenticity and sustainability as a lifestyle. Though it may be a difficult transition at first, choose to spend your money on items that are designed to last, rather than that which is cheap and disposable. Tailor your social media consumption to only let in authentic images and messages. Remove any relationships from your life that are built upon dishonesty. Make plans for your home, your career, your relationships, and your body that can evolve into the long-term. Find your own way to contribute to environmental sustainability, whether it's switching to an electric car, planting more trees in your own backyard, or starting up a recycling initiative in your office.

Whatever you choose to incorporate into your self-care routine, remember to treat it as a priority—not the last thing on your to-do list, which is likely to get edged off when anything unexpected comes up. When you set aside regular time to care for and appreciate yourself, you'll be able to function at an elevated level; more importantly, your ability to connect with others empathically will be strengthened and enhanced by your own self-love.

Origins and History of

The Enneagram

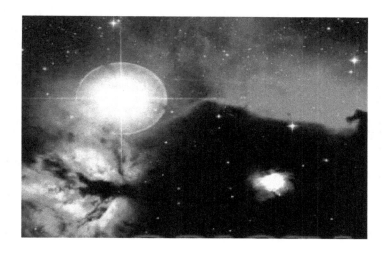

The history of the enneagram, also referred to as the enneagram of

personality types, in modern society can be traced back to Oscar Ichazo and

George Gurdjieff. In the early-mid 1900s, they described how everyone has a unique personality that they identify with within the enneagram. These personalities represent the way we behave, feel and think.

The ancient history of the enneagram is largely undocumented, but it is believed that the concept existed in the Middle East and Asia thousands of years ago. The issue of documentation arises because, during these times, the enneagram was more of a spoken tradition than a written discipline. It is through the works of Ichazo and Gurdjieff, and later on Claudio Naranjo in the 1970s, that the modern concept of the enneagram became popular.

Today many experts have built on this knowledge and presented their own concepts of determining personalities and self-discovery. Some of the terminology used by different experts overlap from one method to another.

Some of the earliest practitioners in the field claimed that their knowledge of the enneagram of personality types was as a result of their interaction with ancient traditions. Because of their inability to prove or authenticate their sources, historical construct of the enneagrams from their perspective has remained ambiguous and has since been largely discarded or disregarded.

George Gurdjieff spent most of his life learning about wisdom, religions, and the traditions that define them. He was an astute businessman, philosopher, and a very spiritual man. During his exploits, Gurdjieff became a teacher, imparting knowledge about human consciousness wherever he went.

According to Gurdjieff, most people do not live to fulfill their purpose in life because while they think they are living, they are actually asleep. He championed the idea that personality and essence are two different things. In his teachings, personalities are learned, which is why it is possible to mimic a personality. On the other hand, the essence is inborn.

Though Gurdjieff is often credited for his role in the development of the enneagram, he never took credit for it. However, he also barely acknowledged any sources. There are many theories about the source of his work, including his interaction with desert mothers and fathers or the Sufis. Some theorists also believe his work might be traced back to theories from ancient Greece.

Whatever the specific inspiration of his work was, the consensus is that most of the work Gurdjieff did towards the enneagram was a result of the interactions he had with people in different environments as he traveled the world.

Ichazo's work picked up from where Gurdjieff left off. His studies were largely influenced by Confucianism and Buddhism, alongside other spiritual affiliations he interacted with. Ichazo wrote several articles on enneagrams, in some of them refuting the earlier claims by Gurdjieff on the sources of his work. According to Ichazo, most of the teachings were picked up from ancient Greek philosophers, the Magi, and some Hindu scriptures. Therefore, it was his belief that Gurdjieff had no role to play in the enneagram, especially since the teachings he publicized were purely universal.

Ichazo then introduced a system which he referred to as protoanalysis, which refers to the methodologies he used in his teachings. In these teachings, Ichazo introduced more than 100 enneagrams.

Building on Ichazo's work came Dr. Claudio Naranjo. Naranjo's work from 1970 was influenced by tragedy when his son died on the eve of Easter. This tragedy forced him on a journey of spiritual discovery, which saw him seek Ichazo's help in Chile. Naranjo proceeded with his studies and discoveries in the field, writing lots of informative books about the enneagram. Since then, interest in enneagrams has grown, with many students trying to expound on the existing knowledge.

Some other notable contributors to the enneagram of personality types include David Daniels, Helen Palmer, Russ Hudson, Don Riso, Theodore Donson, and Kathy Hurley.

Structure of The

Enneagram Diagram

The first step towards understanding the world and people around you is to understand yourself. This is a challenge that many people struggle with. There is a lot that we don't know about ourselves and, with that hindrance, our attempts at understanding other people around us becomes almost impossible. You cannot seek what you don't know, because how will you know that you have found it if you don't know what you were meant to be looking for in the first place?

Understanding the enneagram system will place you on an interesting journey, a journey into self-discovery. The marvels of human nature will enlighten you, astonish you and in some cases probably scare you. You will realize there is much that you never knew about yourself. It will open your eyes to new possibilities and encourage you to recognize your limits, challenges, strengths, and the stimuli in your environment that empower or motivate you.

As you wade through the enneagram, you will learn many things that you can use in your life every day. Like we mentioned earlier, when you learn about yourself, you open your world to new experiences and you learn to understand people better because you look at them from a new enlightened perspective.

Understanding the enneagram structure will introduce positive changes in your life, and give you a new lease of life. The structure of the enneagram might look complex, but it is actually a very simple concept. It features a meshwork of a triangle and an irregular hexagram within a circle. The easiest way to realize the simplicity of this structure is to draw it yourself.

Using a compass, draw a circle. Mark nine points on the circle, each an equal distance away from the other. A circle has 360 degrees, so measure 40 degrees and mark a point, then repeat until you have nine marked along the circumference of the circle.

Label each point with a number, (1 – 9) making sure nine sits at the top. You have now taken the first step towards identifying the nine personality types.

So, before we even consider the triangle or the hexagram, this simple structure already should give you a rough idea of the construct of human personalities. Everything in life comes full circle. Even without digging deep into the theory of the enneagram, you should already be able to surmise the concept of interdependence and the whole.

Once you have completed the enneagram diagram, you will notice that the points are interconnected through smaller lines within the diagram. Take a closer look, and you will notice an equilateral triangle within the circle. This is a triangle with all three sides and angles equal, which is formed by points 3, 6, and 9. The remaining six points interconnect to form an irregular hexagram.

What we can reveal from this diagram is nine different personality types, each connected to each other in some way. What does this tell you about yourself? It is a sign that in the whole you, all the nine personalities might manifest in some way. If you reflect on your life and some of the choices you have made, you should realize that you possess a little bit of every one of them. However, there will be one personality type that stands dominant above the rest. This dominant one is the personality type that defines you. It is the foundation of your being.

Personalities are inborn. They manifest from your childhood and, as you grow older, you embrace your personality type and go on to become the person you are today. Everyone is born with a clean slate. Over the years, many authors and experts on enneagrams have attempted to demystify the concept of personalities. While each expert presents a unique perspective, most believe that everyone is born with a dominant personality type.

This inborn personality becomes your identity. It is through it that you learn how to embrace the environment around you, how to interact with the people you meet, the things you dislike, and activities you are drawn to. The decisions we make are a construct of our subconscious mind. In turn, the subconscious mind is influenced by your dominant personality. This explains why you form some associations with your loved ones and parents, but perhaps have a different perspective of authority and respond differently to affection from other people.

The growth process and personalities are linked. Around the time that children turn six years old, they start to portray unique behavior and responses to different changes in their lives. Their identity starts becoming apparent, and they embrace a new freedom to choose their role in the world.

Generally, the personality type you associate with is a combination of many changes that take place in your life from childhood. Other than genetics, this includes the environment you are brought up in, the defining moments in your life and anything else that may have influenced your growth and development in some way. Because of this, it is safe to say no one is able to just switch their personality from one to another. We all have tiny fragments of all the personality types within us. These manifest differently in the way we respond to different situations in life. This means that it is possible that one of your lesser personalities might suddenly become prominent, perhaps because you find yourself in uncharted territory, as it becomes the only way you can adapt. However, the dominant personality type will always return and persist.

The idea of a dominant personality type can be misleading. By the definition of 'dominant,' you would assume that this particular personality type would dominate your life all the time. However, this is not the case. If you consider all the descriptions and character traits that define your dominant personality type, you will see that it is impossible to manifest all of them all the time. Some of the characteristics may be subtle, whereas others are prominent, so you might not experience the totality of your personality at all times.

Most of the personality traits are expressed in response to someone or something, which we define as a reaction. Your reaction to conflict at home might not be the same as your reaction to conflict at work. The same theory applies to the way you show affection, and how you care for people. Your position or stage in life also influences the way your personality manifests.

Cultural affiliations also have an impact on your personality, because of moral beliefs and the differences in beliefs between cultures. It must be clarified that none of the personalities should be considered superior to the rest. The numerical connotation is simply a neutral designation to eliminate the risk of bias. A number 9 does not mean that this personality is better than a number 3.

There are some traits that each cultural construct holds in high regard. If you demonstrate such traits in your personality, you will be highly favored in these communities. The natural reaction in this scenario will be to embrace the affection and favor, which will, with time, become second nature to you. However, you cannot have too much of anything without some kind of repercussions, right? Take an example of someone who cares deeply about relieving the suffering of others. While you can go out of your way to help people, you can't do it all the time. It will take a toll on you eventually, and while you may be performing an act of kindness, there will be a struggle in other spheres of your life as a result of your good deeds.

The same holds true with personality types. The more you learn about them, the clearer your perception will become. However, awareness of personality types is not complete until you also become aware of their limitations. Personalities and their traits are recommended by different societies in different ways. Does this mean that some personalities are better than others? No, not really. What we can learn from this is that each society has a unique reward scheme that appreciates some traits in some personalities over others.

So where does this leave you, and what can you do about your life? The short answer is self-awareness. Know who you are and what your life is about. Learn about and master the different personality types. Figure out what your personality type is and the characteristic traits that you identify with.

Why is this important? We live in a world where people are struggling to fit in. Thanks to social media, the world is obsessed with appearances, looks and perceptions. Many people live their lives in the shadow of other people, not because they are forced to but because they believe it is the only way to gain fulfillment and satisfaction. This is, however, a fallacy. An imitation by any other name is still just an imitation. Whenever you try to portray yourself as something or someone else, you only succeed at perfecting the lie. With each attempt, you lose grasp of your true self. If you imitate someone for too long, you might end up forgetting your own identity or be ashamed of accepting who you truly are.

Self-awareness is about embracing your true self. You will learn what makes you tick, why you do the things you do and, in the process, learn to appreciate your place in this life. You will understand your value and the value others have in your life.

Discovering Your Personality Type

While we know, there are only nine different personality types; determining the one that best describes you is not that simple. Matters of human personality are not always black and white. As well as the nine main personality types, these are some of the other factors that come into play:

- Subtypes

Within each of the nine personality types, there are three variants. Therefore, in theory, there are 27 different characteristics within which you will be able to identify yours. However, given that some of them share very close similarities, this is not one of the easiest things to do.

- Wings

The term 'Wings' in this discussion refers to the adjacent types on either side of each personality type. As you read further into the personality types, you will learn that each personality associates with at least one of the other adjacent personalities. This association has a profound influence on your life, though it is not as great as the dominant personality type. In some cases, both adjacent personality types can influence your life.

- Arrows/lines

Arrows refer to the direction you expect your characteristic behaviors to take in relation to the world around you, whether you are comfortable or you are under stress.

- Development level

The way your personality type manifests also depends on your level of personal growth and development. Individuals who are developed are usually exposed to different levels of maturity, in which case it becomes difficult to identify which category they belong to. Such individuals can portray different characteristics of each personality because they can draw knowledge from their learned and shared experiences, which means they are able to balance their lives and blend in or adapt to different scenarios comfortably.

Given the challenges above, how can you make sure you have a good shot at learning and embracing your personality type? The following discussion will provide you with everything you need to go about this.

Keep an open mind

From the very beginning, you will need to start by eliminating your personal bias towards the enneagram tests or anything else connected with this process. You need to embrace the tests and take them correctly. Don't hold back when answering the questions. After you have the results and you have an idea of what your dominant personality is, make sure you do not rest on your laurels.

You might notice that something within your behavior that does not conform with what you originally believed. This might change your perception of your personality type, especially if you are already in doubt.

Don't obsess over types!

When you read about the different personality types and their unique features, you may fantasize about certain types under the misconception that they are better than the others. The problem here is that you will lose focus on the important facts. These personality tests are not about the different types; they are about you.

Do not approach this from the perspective of characteristics you wish that you have. You are not assigning yourself a type; you are trying to find out what your type is, based on your current predispositions.

Personal bias

It is common for people to come in with preconceptions about themselves when learning about the enneagram of personality types. Often, they will shy away from revealing some of the traits that they consider to be negative. However without admitting such traits, you won't get a true picture of who you are. Remember that the personality tests can only give an accurate or a near-accurate result if you provide it with accurate data.

The risk of ambiguity

As you learn about the personality types, you must be prepared for some ambiguous results. In particular, the peacemaker and the loyalists are two groups that can be easily confused as most of their traits are relatively universal. They could represent almost every other personality type, so you might have a difficult time pointing them out.

As well as this, these two categories don't have very distinct features that you can identify with. If you already are conflicted about a few of the categories, the ambiguity of the peacemaker and loyalist might confuse you even further.

How to Improve Your Life

For heaven's sake, stand up for yourself. Make a choice. You don't always have to go along with what other people want you to do. When was the last time you did something solely for yourself? Keeping the peace is awesome, but do you know what else is better? Personal satisfaction. Maybe you think that you are happy because you make other people happy, but actually, their happiness has nothing to do with you. It is about their needs being met. You need to start focusing on yourself, by thinking about the things that make you happy, and doing them.

Stop daydreaming. The fantasy world you run off to when things get dark is not real. Everything you need is in this world, so open your eyes and embrace new experiences. Be active, and involve yourself in doing things that add value to your life.

Listen to your feelings. Stop shutting them out just so you can focus on what other people want. Your needs must also be met. The unpleasant feelings are a part of your life, and you must get through them. They challenge your vulnerabilities, but they will also make you stronger because you learn a lot by listening to your pain.

What role did you play in the most recent conflict that hurt you? Perhaps you broke up with your partner, or you are having issues with your colleagues at work. Within human interactions, it is normal for people to get into conflict when one or the other does not feel like they are being appreciated, or that their needs are being met. Don't let the goodness of your actions prevent you from admitting your faults.

Frequently Asked

Questions

1. Why is emotional intelligence receiving so much attention?

For many people, it is clear that classical concepts of definition did not seem to fit their subjective experience of being human. Science can invent highly sophisticated forms of IQ tests that can recognize fine differences in cognitive ability, but that does not necessarily make a statement about the ability of an individual to be successful in a career, in a relationship, or life in general. Studies of emotional intelligence emerged in part because of dissatisfaction with the way that concepts of intelligence (and the associated IQ tests) seemed to fail at capturing what makes people human. As IQ testing became more common in schools and was used to make educational decisions, a search for another way of understanding intelligence, a more accurate way, was needed and thus was the study of emotional intelligence born in the 1960s.

2. What is emotional intelligence?

Emotional intelligence can be tricky to define because different models of EI define this quality differently. This book follows the mixed model of EI, which sees emotional intelligence as encompassing a particularly important range of abilities. These abilities include the following: (1) the capacity of men and women to recognize their own emotional state and the emotional state of others, (2) the capacity to distinguish between different emotions and label these emotions accurately, (3) the capacity to use emotional understanding as a guide for one's cognition and actions, (4) the capacity to modify or manage one's feelings in order to achieve a goal or as part of adaptation to a particular environment.

One model of EI focuses on self-awareness as representative of EI while another pays attention to recognizing emotion in general and acting on this recognition. The mixed model appreciates the relationship that exists between being self-aware, recognizing the emotions of others, and using emotion as a guide for behavior.

3. What is the difference between emotional intelligence and traditional intelligence?

Emotional intelligence emerged at a time when the only understanding of intelligence is what we may think of as traditional intelligence. Now there is the idea of multiple intelligences of which emotional intelligence was one, but 50 years ago the only type of intelligence that science believed in was cognitive ability: the problem solving, spatial reasoning, and related computational skills that are measured by IQ tests.

Now it is understood in many quarters that this concept of cognition as the only type of intelligence is not perhaps accurate as it does not encompass the full range of human abilities and human behaviors. If all human beings did was compute, then we would be a little different from computers with organs. Human beings are from that, and a lot of that has to do with our experience of having feelings and connecting with others through emotion. Emotional intelligence, therefore, is thought by many to exist alongside other forms of intelligence as part of a human skill set necessary for life.

4. How is emotional intelligence measured?

Emotional intelligence is measured by EQ, emotional quotient. There are several major EQ tests, which represent ways of measuring emotional ability in the three different models of EI.

5. What is the relationship between emotional intelligence and empathy?

Many people equate emotional intelligence with empathy. Although this is not completely accurate, it does help some people understand what EI is especially in the context of multiple definitions and understandings of EI. Properly, empathy is one of the components of emotional intelligence, along with self-awareness, self-regulation, motivation, and social skills. The key to understanding EI is the ability to recognize that these components work in tandem to some degree. So someone who has skills in one component of EI may still come across as lacking EI if they are deficient in another area. Therefore, though empathy may help some to understand EI, the reality is that possession of empathy alone would not be sufficient to successfully display and benefit from EI.

6. Are empathy and sympathy the same thing?

Sympathy is oft confused with empathy. The capability of having compassion for others and showing tolerance of them is technically sympathy. Empathy is the ability to feel and share the subjective emotions and experiences of another person. Empathy becomes confused as some definitions of it include compassion as part of the definition. It may be helpful to think of sympathy as being a part of empathy (particularly in the feeling of compassion), but recognizing that empathy extends beyond sympathy to involve the sharing of subjective experience rather than simply feeling compassion for it.

7. Is emotional intelligence acquired in a different way from other forms of intelligence?

The study of intelligence is a field with many theories. Some people believe that intelligence is something that is inherited and that behaviors that are undertaken in life may impact knowledge but would not actually change intelligence. What makes emotional

95

intelligence unique is the recognition that human beings are both born with emotional intelligence to some degree and are capable of acquiring EI throughout their lives.

For some people, this peculiar aspect of EI (that it is both native and learned) is encapsulated in the idea of traits and skills. Men and women may be born with EI traits and may acquire EI skills over time. This certainly is semantics, but it underscores the idea that emotional intelligence can be acquired, making EI something different from some other forms of intelligence like these, as understood today.

8. Can emotional intelligence skills be learned and improved?

The power of EI is that it is not static; at least it doesn't have to be. Emotional intelligence skills can be improved with a thoughtful examination and training. Most people have some skills with emotional intelligence, even if this may not be clear to those interacting with them. For example, most humans are aware to some extent of their own emotions and are able to recognize the emotions of otherwise. Where problems come into play is whether or not this awareness is used to guide behaviors and interactions that follow.

9. What is EQ and is it different from IQ?

EQ is sometimes used synonymously with emotional intelligence (EI), but it actually represents a unique aspect of EI. EQ, or emotional quotient, technically is the measurement of EI, which means that EI is the quality that one is trying to measure, and EQ is how you measure it. The state of affairs with EQ and EI is similar to the situation with IQ and intelligence. IQ (intelligence quotient) is not intelligence, just how intelligence is quantified, although, in common parlance, people often say IQ when they are referring to intelligence.

EQ is different from IQ because emotional intelligence is somewhat more heterogeneous than traditional ideas of intelligence as measured by EQ. Indeed, there is not a consensus on how EI should be defined, which results in a situation where each model of emotional intelligence has its own barrage of EQ tests to measure it. Therefore, though EQ is emotional intelligence's version of IQ,

EQ tests can be drastically different from one another because of different beliefs of what EI is and how it can be measured.

10. Why do human beings demonstrate empathy?

Human beings are an exceptional species, even if we seem not to be doing such a great job with the planet we happen to be living on at the moment. As part of our exceptionality, human beings are able to form deep connections with one another. One of the ways that we do that is by having empathy for one another. If you believe in evolution, then empathy may have developed because it enhanced our survival somehow. Perhaps those ancestors of ours who developed empathy were able to form stronger and more effective social groupings than those who did not. Whatever the case may be, the benefits to humans of empathy are clear, and this trait does not appear to be going anywhere anytime soon.

11. Is there a reason why some people seem to lack skills in emotional intelligence?

What is interesting about emotional intelligence is that it strikes a medium between those skills that might be native to us and those which may be acquired throughout life. Some people are born with great self-awareness, empathy, or self-regulation. Some others may be relatively deficient in these areas and may have to learn and practice them over time. Indeed, there are probably not a lot of people who excel in all components of emotional intelligence. Most people will be lacking in some areas and will require some effort to improve.

It is not easy to state exactly why some people seem to lack EI skills, while others seem not to. The reality is that most people have skills in one of the five areas of emotional intelligence, but because they may lack skills in other components, they come across as lacking EI. For example, someone may have empathy, but they may lack social skills, so their interactions are unsuccessful. As another example, someone may have self-awareness but may lack self-regulation and empathy. Successful EI requires that men and women have some level of proficiency in all areas of EI.

12. What is the role of non-verbal communication in emotional intelligence?

Non-verbal communication is very important in emotional intelligence. Because EI involves being able to recognize emotion accurately, any cue that is an indicator of emotion will necessarily be important in emotional awareness. The reality is that human beings used non-verbal cues to communicate. This is just as true of our primate cousins as it is of us. Non-verbal cues like facial expression, body language, hand position, distance, and the like all indicate our emotional state as well as our willingness to engage with others. Other people use these non-verbal cues to gauge what we are thinking and how we feel about them, so it is in the interest of every person trying to hone emotional intelligence skills to pay attention to those things that are expressed but not actually said.

13. How can developing emotional intelligence skills improve my life?

Emotional intelligence skills are critical to leadership. Indeed, the mixed model of EI defines this quality as a skillset needed by leaders. Leaving aside the executive functions of EI, emotional intelligence also enhances social interaction by improving the abilities of human beings to communicate with each other. This is one of the advantages that emotional intelligence has over traditional understandings of intelligence. Traditional models of intelligence ignore human communication and interaction, an oversight that causes IQ to often be a poor indicator of success. By honing your abilities to recognize emotion and modify your behavior accordingly, you can certainly improve your quality of life.

14. Do I need to develop emotional intelligence skills in order to have a successful life?

Emotional intelligence is not a skill set that men and women should ignore. This spectrum of traits and skills is not something that scientists invented fifty years ago. Studies in EI have attempted to quantify those aspects of humanness that have long been obvious

101

to anyone who was paying attention. Human beings are social animals, which means that skills that facilitate social interaction or lead to better social interaction are critical to being successful as a human being. Even if emotional intelligence is something that you are unfamiliar with and only just now learning about, the evidence suggests that developing EI skills can make the difference in living a life filled with the success that comes from fruitful social interaction.

15. Is emotional intelligence as important as other forms of intelligence?

Emotional intelligence has been studied so actively for the past three decades because its supporters believe that it is just as important as other forms of intelligence, namely cognitive reasoning that is tested with IQ tests. Emotional intelligence is believed to be at least as important as other forms of intelligence because it has been shown to be a primary quality that leaders must have in order to be successful in their roles. Indeed, studies suggest that emotional intelligence, as measured by EQ, is twice as important as EQ in terms of success as a leader.

16. What does artificial intelligence have to do with emotional intelligence?

Technically, nothing, but the manner in which artificial intelligence research and advancements have taken stock of EQ, empathy, and other aspects of emotional intelligence shows that perceptions of the role that feeling has in human ability and human interaction have changed. In the past, intelligence was thought of in terms of pure computational ability or cognition where skills like problem-solving were emphasized. Intelligence and the study of it really had no understanding of the importance of emotion until the 60s and later, when research in emotional intelligence brought these ideas to the forefront.

Now artificial intelligence is expected to understand and demonstrate emotion as a human being would. Artificial intelligence agents are programmed to ask the person they are interacting with how they are and to express emotions (like dismay or sadness) based on the response that they received. This change has occurred because computer scientists and other AI researchers recognize that emotional intelligence and social intelligence as critical aspects of functioning as a human being. As most people who are interacting with AI agents expect the program to behave as a human would, AI advancements have now to focus on humanizing their AI so that it meets a certain standard of humanness.

What this change in this highly computational, scientific field does is recognize that emotion is an essential part of being human. A human being would know that they are dealing with a machine if the other they are interacting with did not express some sensitivity to their emotional state. What this means for the AI of the future is that computer scientists and researchers have to focus on how they can program AI so that it can demonstrate emotion better and learn from its experiences as part of the AI's machine learning capabilities.

17. How does one go about practicing empathy?

The key to empathy is to practice it. This allows individuals with native skills to improve upon them while those without them can develop them over time. Some helpful steps to practicing empathy are: (1) be motivated to have empathy for others, (2) be perceptive of the feelings of others and not just your own, (3) feel compassion for others, (4) talk about the feelings of others, even if it is just talking to yourself, (5) practice caring about the feelings of others rather than just recognizing them.

18. What are some important dates in the history of emotional intelligence?

1964: publication of Michael Beldoch's "Sensitivity to the expression of emotional meaning in three modes of communication."

1966: publication of Leuner's "Emotional intelligence and emancipation."

1983: publication of Gardner's *Frames of Mind: The Theory of Multiple Intelligences*

1985: Payne's dissertation, "A Study of Emotion: Developing Emotional Intelligence."

1989: publication of Greenspan's model of EI

1990: publication of Mayer and Salovey's model of EI

1995: publication of Daniel Goleman's *Emotional Intelligence – Why It Can Matter More Than IQ*

19. What is limbic resonance?

Some researchers believe that there is a pathway in the brain that is responsible for our ability as human beings to have empathy. The concept of limbic resonance identifies a part of the brain that may be responsible for the deep connections that we, as human beings form with others. The limbic system, as this region is called, is the region associated with deep emotions like fear, and with EI skills like empathy. Some researchers believe that a pathway mediated by norepinephrine is critical in our ability to have empathy for other people. A dopamine pathway may be responsible for the emotions of anxiety, fear, and anger.

CONCLUSION

Thank you for reading all this book!

Thank you for making it through to the end of *Empath Healing: The Empath's Survival Guide. Simple And Effective Practices To Become An Energy Healer And Develop Your Mystic Consciousness.* Let's hope it was informative and able to provide you with all of the tools you need to achieve your goals, whatever they may be.

The next step is to start experimenting with various healing methods in order to find one—or several, if you're lucky—that address your needs. It is always advisable to experience any healing practice from the standpoint of a patient, client, or student before jumping into a training program or offering yourself as a healer.

It is also wise to focus on connecting with as many other empaths and alternative healers as you can find, both socially and professionally. There may not be many fellow empaths in your immediate social or professional circles, but I assure you, like-minded spirits are out there, and they are eager to receive and connect with you! Browse online forums, podcasts, and social media platforms; seek out retreats, or find an inclusive spiritual organization in your area; yoga classes attract empaths like moths to a flame. It may take some effort, but once you start to keep an eye out for fellow empaths, you may be pleasantly surprised to find that we are everywhere, and we all want to support your journey to become a healer.

When empaths come together, their combined strength is multiplied exponentially. Though we are gaining recognition in the fields of psychology and science, we still are a minority in the world. We must support each other, empower each other, share our personal stories, and teach each other, to ensure that the light of empathy continues to spread and grow brighter with every passing year.

Finally, if you found this book useful in any way, a review on Amazon is always appreciated! Spread your light and healing energy by ensuring this book finds its way to as many fellow empaths as possible.

You have already taken a step towards your improvement.

Best wishes!

CPSIA information can be obtained
at www.ICGtesting.com
Printed in the USA
BVHW040322120521
607043BV00001B/272

9 781801 878975